SOLVING MYSTERIES WITH SCIENCE

THE LOCH NESS MONSTER

 Raintree

Chicago, Illinois

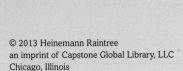

To contact Capstone Global Library please
phone 800-747-4992, or visit our website
www.capstonepub.com

Edited by Adam Miller and Abby Colich
Designed by Marcus Bell
Original illustrations (pages 7, 11, 15) © Chris King
    2013
All other original illustrations © Capstone Global
    Library
Illustrated by Chris King and HL Studios
Picture research by Mica Brancic
Originated by Capstone Global Library, Ltd.
Printed in China by Leo Paper Group

16 15 14 13 12
10 9 8 7 6 5 4 3 2 1

**Library of Congress Cataloging-in-Publication
Data**
Hile, Lori.
  Loch Ness monster / Lori Hile.
      p. cm.—(Solving mysteries with science)
  Includes bibliographical references and index.
  ISBN 978-1-4109-4987-5 (hb)—ISBN 978-1-4109-
4992-9 (pb) 1. Loch Ness monster—Juvenile litera-
ture. I. Title.

  QL89.2.L6H55 2013
  001.944—dc23   2012012695

Acknowledgments

The author and publisher are grateful to the following
for permission to reproduce copyright material:Alamy:
pp. 21 (© Mary Evans Picture Library), 31 (© Lourens
Smak), 33 (© Jim Henderson), 35 bottom (© Stephen
Finn), 40 bottom (© John Robertson), 43 (© 1Apix);
Corbis: p. 18 (© Steve Vidler); Fortean Picture Library:
pp. 37 main, 39; Mirrorpix: p. 27; Newscom: p. 26
(Mirrorpix/Academy of Applied Science Boston
Massachusetts); Photoshot: pp. 20 bottom (© UPPA),
39 (UPPA/© TopFoto); Press Association: p. 25
(Academy of Applied Science Boston Massachusetts/
Robert H Rines); Reuters: p. 36 left (© Jeff J Mitchell
UK); Rex Features: p. 38 main (Daily Mail); Science
Photo Library: pp. 30 (Chris Butler), 32 (Chris Butler),
34 top (Peter Menzel); Shutterstock: pp. 5 (© Ralf
Juergen Kraft), 19 (© Steven Wright), 20 top (©
Phiseksit), 23 (© Jeff Banke), 28 (© Basel101658), 28
(© Eric Isselée), 29 top (© iliuta goean), 29 bottom
(© Hein Nouwens), 34 bottom (© Sashkin), 35 top (©
Megainarmy), 36 right (© Ralf Juergen Kraft), 37 top
(Lisovskaya Natalia), 38 top (© Lindybug), 40 top (©
Smart-foto), 41 top (© Ralf Juergen Kraft); The Kobal
Collection: p. 42 (Beacon Pictures/Blue Star Pictures);
TopFoto: pp. 22 (Fortean Picture Library), 41 main (©
2005 TopFoto/Fortean).

Cover photograph of the Loch Ness monster
reproduced with permission from Shutterestock (©
Victor Habbick).

Design feature images: Shutterstock

Every effort has been made to contact copyright
holders of any material reproduced in this book. Any
omissions will be rectified in subsequent printings if
notice is given to the publisher.

All the Internet addresses (URLs) given in this book
were valid at the time of going to press. However, due
to the dynamic nature of the Internet, some addresses
may have changed, or sites may have changed or
ceased to exist since publication. While the author
and publisher regret any inconvenience this may
cause readers, no responsibility for any such changes
can be accepted by either the author or the publisher.

Contents

Centuries  OF Sightings

Scotland's Loch Ness is dark and deep—the perfect place for a monster to hide! The water in the long, skinny loch (the Scottish-Gaelic word for "lake") is inky-black from peat moss, making it impossible to see more than a few feet beneath the surface.

Does a monster lurk here?

Over the centuries, thousands of people have claimed to see one. The creature even has a nickname: "Nessie." In the first part of this book, we will follow some real-life Nessie stories. In the second part of the book, we will use the scientific method (see page 19) to examine these accounts and help answer the question: Could the Loch Ness monster really exist?

Fast Facts

Loch Ness is only 1 mile (1.6 kilometers) wide, but it is 24 miles (39 kilometers) long, and it is deep enough to house an 80-story building!

Loch Ness is the third deepest lake in Europe.

The loch's temperature is always a chilly 42°F (5.5°C).

Portrait of the Loch Ness monster

Most eyewitness descriptions of the monster include these features:
- a large body with at least one hump
- a long, arched neck and small head
- a gray or brown color.

THE CREATURE WITH THE OVAL EYE

Jim Ayton was tending his father's fields one day when he hollered, "Dad! There's something big moving in the loch!" There, in the middle of Loch Ness, which bordered his father's farm, was a big, black creature. It was swimming silently but swiftly through the deep, dark waters—and heading right toward him!

Jim's father, Hugh, rushed over to look. The lake's surface was as smooth as glass, but halfway across, a massive creature moved steadily in their direction. An eerie hush filled the air. During his 15 years as a farmer, Hugh had heard many rumors about a monster living in the lake, but he had never seen one. Could this mysterious creature be the legendary Loch Ness monster?

Hugh was determined to find out! He quickly rounded up three men, and all four raced down to the dock and squeezed into a small boat. Hugh cranked the motor, and the men began racing toward the strange beast!

CHASING NESSIE

As the men closed in on the creature, Hugh was able to observe it more clearly. Its long, snake-like body

stretched almost 45 feet (14 meters)—the length of a school bus—with several low humps. Its neck curved 6 feet (1.8 meters) into the air, ending with a big, horse-like head with one large eye on top. Its skin seemed dark and rough, like leather.

When the men were just 50 yards (45 meters) away, the beast rose up, its long neck looming over them. Was it going to attack?

> "One thing I will always remember...was an oval-shaped eye near the top of its head, and it looked right at us."
> —Hugh Ayton

The creature splashed headfirst into the water and swirled around, sending the tiny boat spinning with its giant waves. The beast resurfaced farther away, then swam off. Hugh and his soggy crew continued chasing the creature, but they never saw it again.

Although this encounter took place in 1963, Hugh and Jim waited nearly 20 years to report it, because they did not think most people would believe them. But thousands of people have reported seeing strange creatures at Loch Ness over the years.

A FISH STORY?

Retired police officer Ian Cameron was fishing on the south shore of Loch Ness with his friend, Willie Frazer, in June 1965, when Ian saw something rise out of the water, then disappear. "Willie, get over here!" Ian shouted. Ian kept glancing at the spot where he had seen the object. Soon, an enormous black animal shot up from below. The creature looked like a cross between an elephant and a whale!

Willie came rushing over. He had spotted Nessie himself almost exactly a year before. Would he see her again? "Look!" Willie called out. "It's moving toward us." Though the water was flowing in the opposite direction, the giant creature was steadily heading toward the men. The beast came within 250 yards (237 meters) of them, then stopped. But it remained visible for 50 minutes, making it the longest monster sighting on record.

SEEING IS BELIEVING

Dorothy Fraser did not believe in the Loch Ness monster. Although she lived in a cottage overlooking the loch, she had never once seen the monster—and she often told friends that the creature simply did not exist. Then, one spring afternoon in 1967, Dorothy was standing in her garden and gazing out at the lake when she saw a gigantic, gray-black oval mass emerge and start moving through the water. Thinking it might be a submarine, she grabbed her binoculars. That is when she realized it was a huge water creature!

Dorothy's arms and legs grew wobbly and she dropped her binoculars. After taking a minute to calm herself, she watched the beast pick up speed, swimming faster and faster through the lake, until it suddenly disappeared beneath the surface. From that day forward, Dorothy was a Nessie believer.

A FEROCIOUS BEAST?

In 565 CE, a villager was swimming across the Ness River when a humongous beast surged up from below and clasped its giant jaws around the man's body. The beast spit him out, but the man was severely wounded and soon bled to death.

A SLEEPING MONSTER

Saint Columba, an Irish monk (religious man), heard the villagers wailing and moaning as they buried the man. He wanted to comfort the people, but he needed a boat to reach them. Columba asked his faithful servant, Lugne Mocumin, to swim across the river to retrieve a boat anchored on the other side. So Lugne plunged into the river and began paddling.

But Lugne's splash awakened the monster, which was still lurking at the bottom of the river. Annoyed by the disturbance, the beast burst up from below and, with a deafening roar, charged at the man. Its humongous jaws were open wide!

TAMING THE BEAST

Saint Columba shook in anger, realizing that the beast was about to sink its sharp teeth into his loyal servant. Then he raised his hand and shouted, "Thou shalt go no further, nor touch the man; go back with all speed!" Upon hearing the saint, the monster recoiled in fear and fled, according to Saint Columba's biography (life story), "as if it had been pulled back with ropes."

Since then, a water beast has never again harmed a person in the river or the loch it connects to. Some say this is due to the power of the saint's words.

LAND ENCOUNTERS

"Watch out!" cried Mrs. Spicer. She and her husband George, a London businessman, were driving alongside Loch Ness on their way from vacation in July 1933, when she saw a dark shape stretch across the road about 200 yards (182 meters) in front of their car.

A BODY THE SIZE OF A BUS

As they drew closer, the Spicers could see that the object was the arched neck of an enormous creature. Its long, gray neck was connected to an even longer body—the size of a city bus—and shaped like a giant snail. The creature had no arms or legs, but dangling from its mouth was a small animal, like a lamb or rabbit.

> # "It was the nearest (thing) to a prehistoric animal that I have ever seen."
> ## —George Spicer

As Mr. Spicer zoomed forward, the beast lurched across the road in a jerky motion and crashed through some bushes near the loch. When the Spicers reached the bushes, the beast had already slithered into the murky loch and disappeared from sight.

FLATTENED BUSHES

Shaken, the Spicers fled the area and stopped at a nearby village. There, they shared their experience with a local resident, who was amazed to hear their account. He told them that a friend of his had just recently seen a huge creature almost exactly like the one the Spicers described. The man rode his bike to the area where the Spicers had experienced their scary encounter and noticed that the bushes and shrubs were flattened, as if a giant steamroller had crushed everything in its path.

This was one of the first modern Nessie sightings, and it was the first one on land. Afterward, people from around the world started showing interest in Nessie, and huge prizes were offered for her capture.

THE MONSTER AND THE MOTORCYCLE

A full moon hung high in the sky, lighting up the loch and the highway that wrapped around it. This was good news for Arthur Grant, a young student of veterinary (animal) medicine who was returning home on his motorcycle late one January evening in 1934. As Arthur rose up from a dip in the bumpy road, he spotted a large, dark creature crouching near the bushes ahead. Arthur stepped quickly on his brakes to avoid a collision with the animal. But the beast, apparently alarmed by the sound of the cycle, darted through the bushes, toward the loch.

VANISHED INTO THE MIST

Arthur leapt off his motorcycle and scrambled down to the shoreline, just in time to watch the creature plunge into the water with an enormous splash. Arthur peered out into the loch, but the creature seemed to vanish into the night, leaving only moonlit ripples.

> "It looked like...a cross between a plesiosaur and a member of the seal family."
> —Arthur Grant

Arthur rushed home to tell his friends and family about his near-accident with the Loch Ness monster. To preserve his memory, he immediately drew several sketches of the creature. He used his veterinary training to write a detailed account of the animal. He described it as having "a long neck and large, oval-shaped eyes on the top of a small head" and a long, powerful tail, like a kangaroo. According to Arthur, the creature was about 20 feet (6 meters) long and like no animal he had ever seen before.

CRACKLING NOISES

"What's that noise?!" Margaret wanted to know. Margaret Cameron and her brothers and sister were splashing and skipping stones into the loch, when suddenly they heard loud crackling noises coming from the woods nearby. As the sound moved closer and closer, Margaret froze, her heart thumping.

And then she saw it: an enormous creature with shiny, gray skin. The animal was facing Margaret, so she could not see its neck, but she could see its gigantic body. Although her legs were shaking, Margaret dashed out of the beast's path as it lumbered toward the beach. Then, as quickly as it appeared, the animal vanished into the water.

For a moment, Margaret and her siblings could not move. Then, they raced all the way back home, their legs still quivering. There, they all spoke at once:

"Mom! Dad! There was a monster...in the bushes! It ran into the loch! Kind of like an elephant! It was huge!! No, we ALL saw it!"

Their parents looked at each other, then at their kids. Then, they shook their heads and warned the kids never to say another word about the incident, saying, "People will just think you are telling a whopper [lie]!"

A HUGE SECRET

So for years, Margaret kept the story to herself. But decades later, she described the experience, which took place in 1914, to the British Broadcasting Corporation (BBC). She said the event "is still so very vivid in my mind. I'll never forget it."

Like an elephant

In 1879, a group of children was playing in a graveyard on the north shore of Loch Ness when a large animal the color of an elephant came tramping down a hillside. The beast's tiny head swiveled from side to side as it waddled into the water and disappeared. The children reported the strange event to the police.

Investigating the Loch Ness MONSTER

Scotland's Loch Ness has a long history of monster sightings. An ancient people known as the Picts carved pictures of strange water beasts on stones near the loch almost 2,000 years ago (see page 33), and Scots have long told legends about water beasts known as kelpies, which were shape-shifting water horses.

But most of the 9,000 eyewitness sightings that have been written down have occurred more recently, especially after 1933, when a new highway was built around the loch. The new road brought more tourists to the area and opened up better views of the lake…and all the things that lurk in it.

▼ The remains of Urquhart Castle can be seen along the shore of Loch Ness.

Fact or fiction?

What exactly have all of these eyewitnesses seen? A monster? Or is there another explanation? When investigating events or making discoveries, scientists use a process called the scientific method (see the box). In this section of the book, we can use these same steps as we investigate the mystery of the Loch Ness monster.

The scientific method

Good investigators follow the scientific method when they need to establish and test a theory. The scientific method has five basic steps:

1. Make observations (comments based on studying something closely).

2. Do some background research.

3. Form a testable hypothesis. This is basically a prediction or "educated guess" to explain the observations.

4. Conduct experiments or find evidence to support the hypothesis.

5. After thinking carefully about the evidence, draw conclusions.

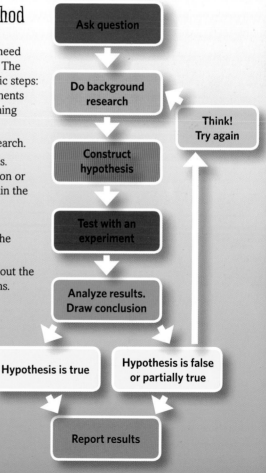

Ask question

Do background research

Construct hypothesis

Test with an experiment

Analyze results. Draw conclusion

Think! Try again

Hypothesis is true

Hypothesis is false or partially true

Report results

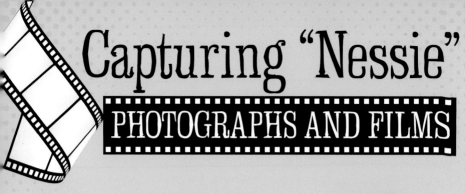

Capturing "Nessie"

PHOTOGRAPHS AND FILMS

"There's a monster living in my bedroom!" If your best friend made this claim, you would probably demand some sort of evidence. Evidence is also necessary for those who claim a monster lives in the loch. Fortunately, several eyewitnesses have snapped photographs and made films of the monster.

Giant monster— or swimming dog?

Late in 1933, an Englishman named Hugh Gray watched a large, gray creature thrashing in the loch. By then, dozens of people had already reported monster sightings, but Gray had something no one else did: a camera. He snapped several photos, and a Scottish newspaper printed one of them. It showed a blurry object in the water.

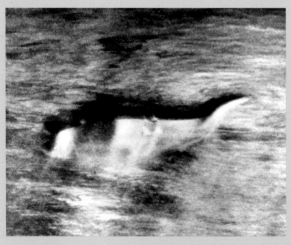

▲ It's difficult to see if this photo, taken by Hugh Gray, contains a monster, a swimming dog, or some other object.

Photography experts believed that the photo was genuine (real). But there are problems with it. For one thing, the photo does not include a shoreline or any landmarks, so there is no way to verify it was even taken at Loch Ness. It is also impossible to determine the size of the object, since there are no other objects in the photo for comparison. Some people think it looks like a dog swimming with a branch in its mouth.

The "surgeon's photo"

In April 1934, a much clearer photo was published. A respected London surgeon named Robert Wilson submitted this one. The photo, which became known as the "surgeon's photo," showed a creature with a long neck and small head rising out of the loch.

Some scientists believed that the photo depicted a large creature with a 4-foot- (1.2-meter-) long neck. But some skeptics were not so sure. Instead of a large, faraway object, they thought it could be a close-up of a small object, like a waterbird, otter, or log. But most scientists accepted the photo as one of the best pieces of evidence for Nessie—until many years later (see page 39).

▼ For years, this image—known as the "surgeon's photo"—provided the best evidence for the Loch Ness monster.

A huge, moving creature

One person completely convinced by the "surgeon's photo" was a young man named Tim Dinsdale. After carefully studying the image, he came to the conclusion that all of the details—including the ripples in the water—looked consistent with the body of a big monster. Inspired, Dinsdale dedicated his life to finding Nessie.

In 1960, on his first expedition, Dinsdale saw a huge, oval-shaped object out in the loch. Through his binoculars, he could see the object rolling around in the water, and he knew it must be a living creature! He grabbed his movie camera and filmed the creature's zigzag movements for four minutes, before it disappeared underwater.

"Before I saw the film, I thought the Loch Ness monster was a load of rubbish [garbage]. [Now] I'm not so sure."

—*the computer technician who enhanced Dinsdale's film*

Was it Nessie?

The United Kingdom's Joint Air Reconnaissance Intelligence Center (JARIC) analyzed Dinsdale's film and came to the conclusion that the object in the water was probably a living creature that was about 12 to 16 feet (3.6 to 4.8 meters) in length. It was 3 feet (1 meter) above water, moving at 10 miles (16 kilometers) per hour.

Beast or boat?

But some researchers were skeptical (not convinced) and decided to analyze the film themselves. When they made some adjustments to the film's settings, they found that the object resembled a small boat—with a human on board. But in 1993, other researchers used a computer to enhance the film. They found that the object had a shadow that resembled the rear body of a plesiosaur (an aquatic relative of the dinosaur), with two humps and two flippers!

Scientists still disagree on exactly what Dinsdale's film shows, but almost everyone agrees that it remains an important piece of evidence.

▼ Could a boat, steaming down Loch Ness, have been mistaken for a monster?

Beneath THE Surface

STROBE LIGHTS _AND_ SONAR SEARCHES

The photographs and film did not provide positive proof of the monster. So researchers decided to seek Nessie where she surely spent most of her time—underwater!

Strobes, sonar, and snapshots

The lake has always been difficult to search. Peat moss clouds the water and blocks light from reaching more than a few feet down. But an American named Robert Rines was prepared. For his first expedition in 1972, he fitted boats with super-strong lamps called strobe lights as well as underwater cameras.

How does sonar work?

Deep in the sea there is almost no light. But there is sound. This is why scientists use sonar, which sends out waves of sound to locate underwater objects. Scientists can determine how far away an object is by how long it takes for the sound to bounce back. They can also calculate how big an object is by counting how many echoes they receive.

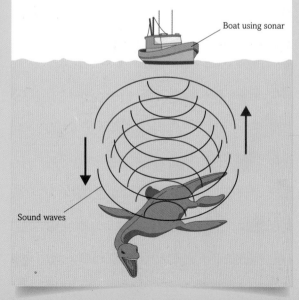

Boat using sonar

Sound waves

He also linked the cameras to sonar devices. These devices send bursts of sound underwater. When the sound strikes an object, it bounces back (see the box). If the device were to detect a big or unusual object, the cameras would automatically start snapping photos.

The flipper

Late one night, the sonar started beeping. It had located a large, moving object! At the same time, salmon started leaping near the surface, as though they were fleeing from a large animal. That is when the camera, which was suspended 45 feet (14 meters) underwater, captured an amazing image. After the photo was enhanced by a computer, it showed what looked like a huge flipper that was about 8 feet (2.4 meters) long and 4 feet (1.2 meters) wide. Any animal with a flipper that large would have to be huge—maybe 30 feet (9 meters) or more long!

▼ This photo, snapped below the surface of the loch during Robert Rines's 1972 expedition, resembles the fin of a large animal.

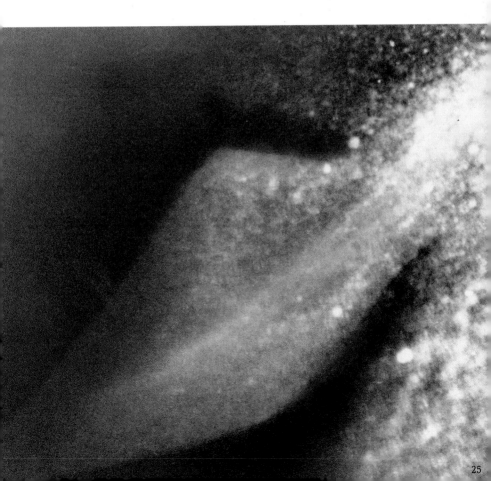

The body of the beast?

Rines led another sonar expedition in 1975. This time, the camera snapped an even more amazing photo—what looked like a large creature with a long neck, small head, and front flippers. Like the shadow in Dinsdale's film (see pages 22 and 23), the image resembled a plesiosaur!

▼ Captured during Robert Rines's 1975 expedition, this underwater photo seems to feature a plesiosaur, a creature thought to be extinct.

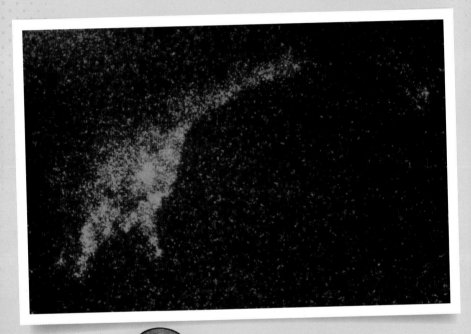

The monster's head?

A second photo, which became known as the "gargoyle photo," seemed to show a wrinkled, horse-like head with two small horns. Could it be the monster's head?

Beast or bubbles?

Some scientists were convinced that a family of large, unknown animals lived in the loch. But others came to a different conclusion. Because the sonar photos were fuzzy, they said the images could easily depict more common objects. For instance, they believed the image of the monster's body was simply small gas bubbles in an air sac. And they thought that the gargoyle head might be nothing more than a rotting tree stump or rusted engine block.

Sonar skeptics

Skeptics also raised doubts about Rines's flipper photo after they saw that the original photo looked very different from the one that was published. Rines said that the published photo simply combined several versions of the original photo. But skeptics argue that Rines specifically emphasized features that made the image look more like a flipper. They also noted that, when the flipper photo is turned sideways, it does not even resemble a flipper.

Since then, there have been several other sonar expeditions. Some have resulted in unexplained sonar strikes. One of them revealed the true identity of the strange gargoyle head—it was indeed just a rotting tree stump! But none of them provided positive evidence of Nessie.

▼ A newspaper displays an image of the famous "gargoyle photo," originally believed to be the monster's head.

SUNDAY MAIL, December 14, 1975   11

THE LOCH NESS FILE

THE GARGOYLE

IN COLOUR

The Mail told you about this picture first

An artist's impression of the picture above.

THIS IS IT! In full colour, the picture that has set the whole world talking. And the picture that has flung the scientific world into total confusion.

Judge for yourself—is it or is it not a photograph of Nessie?

● Three weeks ago the Sunday Mail was the FIRST newspaper in the world to reveal its existence.

● We were the FIRST newspaper in the world to describe it in detail.

By JAMES LAING

● Now for the FIRST time, in any newspaper, we show it in colour.

IS IT OR IS IT NOT A PHOTOGRAPH OF THE LOCH NESS MONSTER?

SLIDES

Dr Robert Rines, the American scientist-lawyer who took it is convinced it is. So too is naturalist Sir Peter Scott.

There is no doubt that the picture shows something—a gargoyle head emerging from the murky waters of the loch.

It is just as it was described by author Nicholas Witchell in the Sunday Mail after he had flown to Dr Rines' home in Boston, Massachusetts, to view the slides.

"The head was ugly. Gargoyle was the word that came to mind. It was hideous, angular, bony and revolting."

The picture also seems to show a bony ridge across what appears to be a snout. There is a mouth, a neck and something like two stalks on top of the head.

It was *this* picture and a series of others which were shown to a gathering of scientists and MPs

the House of Commons on Wednesday last week.

And at once, controversy arose.

Sir Peter Scott is totally convinced. He has dubbed the monster *Nessiteras Rhombopteryx* which means Ness monster with a diamond fin.

FENCE

One MP, Mr Michael Clark Hutchison, Tory, South Edinburgh, thought the pictures were "absolute rubbish."

But Scottish Under Secretary Hugh Brown said he was passing the information on to fishing scientists at the Scottish Office.

He was more convinced that there

27

What Could It Be?

Since we do not have solid evidence for a large, unknown creature in Loch Ness, maybe we should look at creatures already known to exist. Is it possible that any of these creatures could have been mistaken for the Loch Ness monster? The following are some possibilities, all known to live in or around the loch.

Possible animals	Why it could be...	Why it could not be...
Birds	• Many waterbirds have long, curving necks. • When taking off in the water, their wing tips can leave behind a big wake, which could resemble monster humps. • Geese swimming in a line might be mistaken for a many-humped monster.	Waterbirds are much smaller than the creature reported by most observers.
Eels	• When eels poke their head and part of their body out of the water, it can look like a long neck and small head. • When they swim, they move their bodies from side to side, like a snake—which can look like humps.	Eels only reach about 5 or 6 feet (1.5 or 1.8 meters).
Deer	• Deer are good swimmers. In water, the gap between their head and back section can look like a hump. • Young roebucks sprout tiny, knobby antlers, which could be mistaken for the horned head of a monster.	Deer are fairly common and easy to recognize.
Otters	• These furry, brown critters can swim quickly. When they tread water, they stick their head and neck up, like the creature in the "surgeon's photo" (see page 21). • Otters catch animals in their mouth, which would explain the creature the Spicers saw (see pages 12 and 13).	Otters only stay underwater for a few minutes at a time, so they should be frequently seen—and recognized.
Seals	• These large, slick, dark-brown or black creatures can move quickly through the water and even crawl on land.	Seals rarely visit the loch and usually sun themselves out in the open.

Cases of mistaken identity

In 1962, two researchers on an expedition at Loch Ness counted the number of times their crew members mistook other animals or objects for the monster. Out of 16 cases of "mistaken identity," eight were waves, six were birds, one was an otter, and one was a salmon.

▲ From a distance, this long-necked bird known as a cormorant could be mistaken for a long-necked monster.

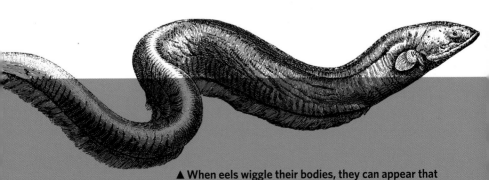

▲ When eels wiggle their bodies, they can appear that they have humps like a monster.

Is Nessie a plesiosaur?

One creature seems like a near-perfect match for the eyewitness descriptions. The creature has a very long neck with a small head. It has a 40-foot (12-meter) body with an oval-shaped stomach, a hump, and a pointed tail. It eats fish and survives in freshwater. And some scientists think it can crawl on land. This creature is the plesiosaur, an aquatic (water-based) relative of the dinosaur.

There is one problem with this idea, however— plesiosaurs are extinct (they died out). Or are they?

▼ Long believed to be extinct, the plesiosaur—a water relative of the dinosaur— most closely fits the description of Nessie.

Fossil chain

The most recent plesiosaur fossil we have is 65 million years old. If plesiosaurs still exist, it seems that more recent fossils would have been discovered. But some Nessie hunters point out that the coelacanth, a huge prehistoric fish, was also believed to have become extinct 65 million years ago. Then, in 1938, the coelacanth was found alive and well off the coast of South Africa. If the coelacanth is still around, why not the plesiosaur?

Getting in

If plesiosaurs do lurk in the loch, how did they get in? The loch was formed just 10,000 years ago, after a glacier melted. This means that the plesiosaurs would have had to survive for 65 million years in the ocean nearby—probably the frosty North Sea—until the Ice Age ended. Then, they would have had to swim through a narrow passage to the loch, becoming trapped there after it was mostly sealed off from the ocean. This is very unlikely, but possible.

▼ Believed to be long extinct, a giant fish called the coelacanth was discovered in 1938. Could the plesiosaur still exist, too?

How many "Nessies" are necessary?

One thing is certain. Nessie could not be 10,000 years old! If these creatures have survived since the loch was formed, a whole family of plesiosaurs must have reproduced (had babies) and died many times over the years. Scientists estimate that at least 10 to 20 plesiosaurs would be necessary to ensure their survival.

There are probably enough fish in the loch for 20 monsters to eat, but if 10 or 20 large plesiosaurs live there, shouldn't we see them frequently? Since plesiosaurs breathed air, they would need to poke their heads out of the water many times a day—which would create a lot of opportunities for sightings if there were many of them.

Don't crane your neck

We picture plesiosaurs with long, curved necks, like the creature in the "surgeon's photo" (see page 21). But some scientists say that the plesiosaur's neck bones were strung together too closely to allow it to bend much. And even if it could, the weight of the long neck would probably topple the entire beast. Instead of sticking their necks way out of the water like a swan or giraffe, plesiosaurs more likely reached them down into the water to gather fish.

LOCH LEGENDS:
A Pictish beast?

The Picts, an ancient people who lived in northern Scotland from 100 to 840 CE, carved beautiful, detailed symbols into stones. The most common symbol, sometimes called the Pictish Beast, is an unknown animal unique to the Picts. It has a long, pointed snout, a spout on the top of its head, and a flipper. Could this be an early illustration of Nessie? Or was this water beast simply a figment of the Picts' imaginations?

Other explanations

But perhaps Nessie is not a creature at all. There are plenty of other possible explanations.

▼ An earthquake fault similar to this one lies under the surface of Loch Ness.

Blame it on the fault

The Great Glen Fault runs the entire length of Loch Ness. The energy released by even a small earthquake could produce low waves in the water, which might resemble the humps of an animal. In 2001, scientist Luigi Piccardi noted that most of the Nessie sightings have taken place directly over the fault line.

"Waking" the monster

If a boat sped down the center of the narrow loch, the wake from the boat would hit both shores at the same time. These waves would then bounce back and crash into each other in the center of the loch, creating a large, hump-like wave. In stormy weather, the wake would be broken up by other waves. But on calm days, the boat wake could last for hours and perhaps fool people into seeing a monster.

▼ Wakes stirred up by boats can last for hours, fooling people into seeing humped creatures.

A vision from the dark side?

Despite so many sightings, Nessie has always been hard to capture on film. This might just be bad luck, but some Nessie researchers have a different explanation. They believe that, instead of a real monster, Nessie is a psychic phenomenon. This means she is something outside the laws of science that cannot be explained by the five senses. The loch does have a history of mystical practices, including demon (devil) worship. Some believe that visions of a "monster" are a result of these evil practices. More likely, though, the loch just feels eerie because it is often murky and gray.

Mistakes AND Hoaxes

Some monster sightings may be cases of mistaken identity. But others are the result of deliberate hoaxes.

Nessie's backbone?

In 2003, Scotsman Gerald McSorley fell into the loch after tripping on an unusual fossil. McSorley brought the fossil to scientists at the National Museum of Scotland, who determined that it was four perfectly preserved bones from a plesiosaur. For McSorley, this was all the proof he needed for Nessie's existence! But even though the fossil was real, it was encased in limestone, a type of rock not found in the loch. Scientists believe that someone planted the fossil near the loch, hoping that it would be discovered and used as proof for the existence of the Loch Ness monster.

Setting up shop

When British photographer Frank Searle set up a tent near Loch Ness in 1969, many people believed he was a serious monster hunter. In fact, a group of people called the Loch Ness Investigation Bureau lent him a camera, and within five years, Searle had published over 20 monster photos. He gained international attention and began selling postcards on a remote shore of Loch Ness. But true Nessie hunters were furious when they learned in 1976 that Searle had faked the photos, creating models of the monster with fence posts, logs, tree branches, and old socks.

▼ Do you think this photo is a hoax, or a picture of the Loch Ness monster?

Wooden beast

In 1958, visitors were startled to see a monster floating calmly in the loch. They did not realize that some mischievous Boy Scouts had built this "monster" from canvas and wood.

The hippo hoax

After Hugh Gray's monster photo was published in 1933 (see page 20), people were hungry for more information about the mysterious beast. One newspaper even hired a professional hunter named Marmaduke "Duke" Wetherell to track down the monster.

After only 48 hours, Wetherell discovered huge, fresh footprints leading to the loch! Wetherell made plaster casts of the prints and sent them to experts at the British Museum in London, England. Their conclusion was that the prints had been made by a right foot of a hippopotamus. Some people believe that local teenagers planted the tracks using an umbrella stand, as such stands were commonly made from dried hippo feet at the time. Wetherell was humiliated.

▼ Marmaduke "Duke" Wetherell prepares to hunt for Nessie in Loch Ness. After being the victim of a hoax, Duke created a hoax of his own.

The "surgeon's photo": An April Fool's Day hoax?

The "surgeon's photo" (see page 21) was published a few months later, but it was not until 1993 that the truth about the photo was revealed. Two Nessie researchers heard rumors that Duke Wetherell had created a phony Nessie photo as revenge for the hippo hoax. Wetherell had died, so they tracked down his stepson, Christian Spurling.

Double hoax?

Not everyone believes the "surgeon's photo" is a fake. Some have questioned why the researchers waited until after Spurling died to announce his confession, making it impossible for others to confirm his story.

Spurling confessed that he had helped his stepfather fake the famous "surgeon's photo." He said that he and Wetherell had mounted a model head and neck onto the top of a 2-foot (0.6-meter) toy submarine.

After photographing it in the loch, they convinced Wilson, a respected doctor, to submit the photos to the newspaper. At the time, few noted the date that Wilson delivered the photos—April 1, 1934. Together, they may have accomplished the biggest April Fool's Day hoax in history.

▲ Would you have believed these photos were of the Loch Ness monster if you saw them in the newspaper?

Mistakes

Hoaxes may account for some monster sightings. But it is also important to consider that eyewitness accounts themselves are not always reliable.

Fake out

In 2005, a historian named Richard Frere proved this when he played a trick on Loch Ness motorists. Frere and a friend pulled off the road and started snapping photos of the loch. After some boats stirred up big waves, Frere started waving and pointing to the loch. Motorists stopped to look. When Frere told them that he saw dark humps out in the lake, about three-quarters of the motorists agreed with him! When asked what he saw, one young boy even sketched a picture of a plesiosaur.

▲ Our eyes can play tricks on us, especially when objects resemble things we want to see.

Power of suggestion

These motorists were not lying. But they also did not see a monster's humps. They only thought they did because Frere suggested it. Our hopes also play a big role in what we see.

For instance, on his first expedition, Nessie hunter Tim Dinsdale saw two big, gray humps about 300 yards (275 meters) from the shore, and he grabbed his movie camera. But when he peeked through his binoculars, he noticed a twig sprouting out of the right "hump." Dinsdale's "monster" was really a tree trunk! If Dinsdale had not had binoculars with him, he probably would have reported the log as a "monster."

Do my eyes deceive me?

Eyewitnesses can also make errors when trying to estimate the size, distance, and speed of objects they see. And some witnesses simply exaggerate their stories to make them more convincing or exciting. For instance, the Spicers (see pages 12 and 13) originally reported that the creature they saw was about 6.5 feet (2 meters). But after a few months, the creature in their story grew to 29 feet (8.8 meters) and then 40 feet (12 meters).

▶ Even legendary Nessie hunter Tim Dinsdale once mistook a tree trunk for Nessie!

41

The Final Report

Although there have been many monster sightings, there is no reason to believe that all of them had the same cause. Perhaps some observers saw otters, others saw waves, and still others saw boats. That would explain why descriptions of the monster differ. It is also possible that some witnesses saw a large, unknown animal.

But to prove that such a creature exists, more evidence is needed. Convincing evidence would include a clear, convincing photo, a positive sonar reading, or the body or bones of the actual beast. Until then, the existence of the Loch Ness monster will remain unproven.

▼ This image from the feature film *Water Horse: Legend of the Deep* imagines the origins of the Loch Ness monster.

$40 million monster

Whether or not the monster exists, sightings continue to capture the imagination of people everywhere. Every year, tourists spend over $40 million on Loch Ness hotels as well as Nessie-themed museums, boat rides, and souvenirs. In 2000, the region installed webcams around the lake so that any Nessie sightings could be captured. Although nothing unusual has yet been caught on camera, the webcams keep the legend alive, reminding people that a monster just might be lurking in the loch!

"Only by draining the loch could it ever be proved that no such animal exists."

—*British scientist Peter Scott, 1976*

▲ Scotland's Loch Ness region strives to keep the Loch Ness monster legend alive with Nessie statues and souvenirs.

Is the Loch Ness monster extinct?

Some researchers believe that the Loch Ness monster once existed, but it became extinct recently, due to food shortages or climate changes. This would explain why the number of Nessie sightings has decreased in recent years. In the 1960s and 1970s, there were dozens of sightings per year. In 2007, there were only two, and in 2010, there was just one. In an age when almost everyone has a cell phone camera, it seems that if Nessie still existed, someone would snap a good photo.

Timeline

65 million years ago
Plesiosaurs are believed to become extinct.

2.58 million years ago
The most recent Ice Age begins.

10,000 years ago
Loch Ness is formed after a glacier melts. The Ice Age ends.

565 CE
Irish Saint Columba is said to have calmed a giant beast in the Ness River.

1879
A group of schoolchildren spots a large, gray animal with a tiny head as it waddles down a hillside and into the loch.

early 1900s
Margaret Cameron and her siblings are scared when an enormous, gray creature crawls out of the woods and into the loch.

July 1933
Mr. and Mrs. George Spicer see a large, long-necked creature on the road that escapes into the loch before they can reach it.

November 1933
A Scottish newspaper publishes the first-ever photo of "Nessie."

December 1933
Marmaduke "Duke" Wetherell finds huge, fresh footprints near the loch.

January 1934
Wetherell's "monster" footprints are revealed to actually be prints from a hippopotamus's foot.

Veterinary student Arthur Grant nearly collides with a large creature on the highway near Loch Ness.

April 1934
The famous "surgeon's photo"—which seems to depict a long-necked creature—is published, inspiring many to search for Nessie.

1938
The coelacanth is discovered off the coast of South Africa.

1958
A group of Boy Scouts floats a "monster" made out of canvas and wood around the lake, fooling many observers.

1960
Tim Dinsdale films a large, black, oval-shaped moving object in the loch.

1963
Jim and Hugh Ayton see a large, long-necked, one-eyed monster from their farm and chase it in a boat.

1965
Two friends spot Nessie while fishing, in what becomes the longest Nessie sighting in history (50 minutes).

1967
Dorothy Fraser, a Nessie skeptic, is converted after seeing something large moving in a loch.

1969–1975
Photographer Frank Searle sets up camp near Loch Ness and sells postcards of his many "monster" sightings, which are only later revealed to be hoaxes.

1972
Robert Rines begins his first sonar expedition, which produces a photo of a very large, flipper-like object.

1975

Rines's second sonar expedition produces two more photos—one of a plesiosaur-shaped image and one of a horse-like head.

1976

Some scientists are convinced by Rines's photos, but others believe they probably depict common objects.

1984

A Nessie skeptic named Maurice Burton analyzes Dinsdale's film and comes to the conclusion that the object in it is actually a boat and a human sailor.

1987

Operation Deepscan is launched, in which a team of boats sweeps every square inch of the loch. There are a few unexplained sonar hits, and the horse-like head is revealed to be a rotting tree stump.

1993

Discovery Communications analyzes Dinsdale's film and finds a plesiosaur-shaped shadow.

Researchers David Martin and Alastair Boyd reveal that the famous "surgeon's photo" was a hoax, after talking with Duke Wetherell's stepson.

2000

Webcams are installed around the lake, to capture all monster sightings and stream live footage around the world.

2003

Gerald McSorley finds four perfectly preserved bones from the backbone of a plesiosaur. Although this raises the hopes of Nessie fans, the bones are found to almost certainly be from the ocean.

The BBC conducts a full-scale sonar scan of the lake, but it finds no large animals.

Summing Up the Science

When people think of the Loch Ness monster, most people think of a plesiosaur. But why?

A plesio-what?

Before 1933, only a few scientists had heard the word "plesiosaur." Interest in these large reptiles grew after eyewitnesses such as the Spicers and Arthur Grant described encounters with prehistoric-looking water beasts. After studying hundreds of eyewitness accounts, Nessie hunter Tim Dinsdale concluded that the creature in Loch Ness was, "without a doubt, a plesiosaur." Later, English naturalist Sir Peter Scott drew a picture of two plesiosaurs roaming the sea. This is the image most people still have of "Nessie."

Hot-blooded?

But could a cold-blooded reptile actually survive in the chilly loch? In short, no. A reptile's body would plunge to the same temperature as the frigid loch and quickly freeze to death. However, scientists now believe that some dinosaurs were warm-blooded. If that is the case, plesiosaurs may have found a way to adjust to the cold temperatures by developing a layer of fat, similar to whales. But other factors still make it unlikely that Nessie really is a plesiosaur.

Glossary

air sac tiny sac in the lungs where oxygen enters and carbon dioxide is released

analyze to examine something carefully

coelacanth large, bony fish thought to be extinct before being found living off the coast of Africa in 1938

conclusion decision that is made after gathering and testing evidence

eerie strange and scary

enhance make better; improve in quality

evidence information and facts that help to prove something

expedition journey or search with a specific goal

extinct having no living members

fault fracture in a rock formation caused by a shifting of Earth's crust

fossil remains or imprint (in a bone, shell, or rock) of a living creature from another time period

gargoyle person or decoration with a strange or ugly appearance

glacier large, slow-moving mass of ice formed over many years from packed snow

hoax trick

hypothesis explanation for an occurrence or problem that needs evidence or testing before it can be accepted as true

Ice Age cold period during which glaciers cover much of Earth. The most recent Ice Age ended 10,000 years ago.

kelpie evil water spirit from Scottish legend, usually having the shape of a horse and causing people to drown; also called a water horse

loch another word for "lake" (from the Scottish-Gaelic)

naturalist someone who studies nature

peat moss dark green or brown growth usually found in wet places

plesiosaur extinct marine (water) reptile with a small head on a long neck, a short tail, and four paddle-shaped limbs. It was alive during the time of the dinosaurs.

prehistoric belonging to a time period before recorded history

saint person seen as good or holy

scientific method process of investigation in which a problem or question is identified, and then experiments are conducted or evidence is found to solve the problem or answer the question

skeptic someone who doubts information or beliefs that others accept

sonar method of detecting, locating, and determining the speed and depth of objects through the use of reflected sound waves

wake visible track of waves left by something moving in water, such as a boat

webcam camera that transfers images to the World Wide Web for others to view

Find Out More

Books

Emmer, Rick. *Loch Ness Monster: Fact or Fiction?* (Creature Scene Investigation). New York: Chelsea House, 2010.

Kallen, Stuart. *The Loch Ness Monster* (Mysterious and Unknown.). San Diego: ReferencePoint, 2009.

Miller, Karen. *Monsters and Water Beasts: Creatures of Fact or Fiction?* New York: Henry Holt, 2007.

Parks, Peggy J. *The Loch Ness Monster* (Mysterious Encounters). Detroit: KidHaven, 2007.

Web sites

www.lochness.com/loch-ness-web-cam.htm
Enjoy the world's first live-streaming webcam overlooking Loch Ness.

www.nessie.co.uk/index.html
This is the official Loch Ness monster site, with up-to-date information on new and past sightings.

www.pbs.org/wgbh/nova/lochness/
A companion to the Nova documentary *The Beast of Loch Ness*, this site offers vivid eyewitness accounts in the witnesses' own words.

www.unmuseum.org/nlake.htm
Learn about famous lake monsters in North American lakes.

Films

The Beast of Loch Ness (PBS, 1999; 2006)
This fun, informative documentary includes eyewitness accounts, a sonar expedition with Robert Rines, and more about the history and mystery of the monster.

In Search of History: The Loch Ness Monster (The History Channel, 2005)
See eyewitness accounts from Russell Flint, who collided with a huge animal in the middle of the lake, and Tim Dinsdale, who inspired many with his film of the monster. Learn the results of several underwater explorations.

The Water Horse: Legend of the Deep (Sony, 2008)
This story, in which a young boy finds a large egg that hatches into a water beast, imagines the origins of the Loch Ness monster.

Index